THE GHOSTS OF
CUMBRIA

LAURIE KEMP

BOOKCASE
2005

COPYRIGHT LAURIE KEMP 2005
PHOTOGRAPHS COPYRIGHT CUMBRIAN NEWSPAPERS
PUBLISHED BOOKCASE 17-19 CASTLE STREET CARLISLE CA3
8SY
WWW.BOOKSCUMBRIA.COM
ISBN 190414708 9

Contents

The Author

Laurie Kemp first came to Cumbria in 1955 to join The Carlisle Journal. Later he worked for Cumbrian Newspapers becoming one-time editor of The Cumbrian Gazette and launch editor of the original series of Cumbrian Life.

He has always been fascinated by the county's history and the characters who, over the years, have played their part in its life. The majority of the stories were first published in Cumbria Life, whose present-day editor, Keith Richardson, commissioned them.

Acknowledgments

Thanks must go to Keith Sutton, Editor of The Cumberland News and The News and Star, for permission to use photographs taken by his photographic staff and to Picture Editor, Mike Scott. The cameramen were Loftus Brown, Phil Rigby, Stewart Blair, Ian Cooper and freelance George Carrick.

Calgarth Hall

A great oak beam ran the length of the room, decorated with carved vine leaves and a cluster of grapes.

The banqueting hall, on the ground floor, was paved with large black oak slabs, mullioned windows were decorated with the arms in stained glass of Miles Phillipson, Kt., and his wife, Janet Laborne.

A spacious chimney had a low, broad, Tudor arch carrying the coat of arms of the Phillipson family - three boars heads with a bend surmounting them, as well as a family shield decorated with a dragon and carrying the motto of former lords - Fide Non Fraude.

What better place, in the Cumberland of the sixteenth and seventeenth centuries, for the lord of the manor to invite guests for nights of entertainment, feasting and merrymaking.

But no! It was haunted! HIGH JINKS WOULD GIVE WAY TO HIGH PITCHED SCREAMS AS LADIES, LIFTING THEIR BROCADED GOWNS, FLED AT THE SIGHT OF TWO SKULLS THAT APPEARED FROM NOWHERE!

No matter that the skulls were thrown into the lake, buried on the mountains, or thrown into lime pits, they always reappeared in the niche at the top of the stairs. Time and time again their groans disturbed the household.

In those early, restless days of border warfare there was a drawbridge across the moat - Calgarth was a fortified house built round a quadrangle - and the main entrance was a broad arched portal defended by a portcullis.

A formidable fortress maybe - but it could not keep out the screaming skulls!

In her book "How Will It End?" published in 1865 and based heavily on the Phillipson family and their relatives the Briggs, prolific author Agnes Strickland uses the local legend of the haunted hall. She has her heroine, Althea Woodville, dozing off in the drawing room, woken by a sudden sound.

"There was nothing alarming in the noise, which was so trifling as hardly to startle her; but a sudden dimness coming over the candles, she looked up to discover the cause of it, and with terror which may be better imagined than described, she perceived two human skulls lying on the little table close to her."

Althea averted her eyes and fainted. The Agnes Strickland story went on: "When Mrs Kezia Briggs, her brother, and Master Elkanah Hobbs (a Puritan Minister) entered the drawing room on their return from chapel they were not a little surprised to find that Althea had fallen from her chair and lay in a deep swoon upon the g round."

When Althea recovered consciousness she exclaimed: "Where are they? How came they there?"

"What do you mean, cousin Woodville?" asked Mrs Kezia.

"The skulls!" cried Althea, shuddering and hiding her face in Mrs Kezia's sleeve.

Mrs Kezia tried to convince Althea that she was dreaming, but the maids attending the ladies would have none of it.

Judy, the head housemaid, exclaimed: "How can you talk at that rate Mistress, when thee knowest fu' w ell that strange lady might have seen the real awfu' skulls of Calgarth!"

"Ay, ay, strange Lunnon lady ha' seen the t'skulls of Calgarth, that be mortal plain truth", echoed all the other damsels in a breath."

The author blames Roundhead officer Colonel Bartholomew Briggs for the apparition - having had two Cavalier supporters unfairly executed - but the local legend that has survived over the centuries

8

has it that the haunting really started with a courtroom drama at the Appleby Sessions.

The woman, white-faced and trembling, had just been condemned to death.

From the dock she stretched a shaking hand, pointed a finger at the magistrate and shrieked a curse: "Harks to here, Myles Philipson, that teenie lump o' land is t'dearest grund a Philipson has ever bowte. For ye shall prosper niver maur, yersel, nor yan o't breed. And while Calgarth's strong woes shall stand, we'll haunt it day and neet!"

It was just one of seven curses that Dorothy Cook laid on Calgarth Hall, home of the Philipson family since 1332, before she and her husband Kraster were led away to await execution.

They had been tried, condemned to death, and were eventually hanged at Appleby.

Their crime? The alleged theft of a silver cup. Legend has it that the curse was laid on Myles Philipson because it was he who had rigged the charge.

Although a large landowner, he had wished to add to his estate a small tenement owned by the Cooks, but they refused to sell. The wicked Myles, claiming that he had no hard feelings, invited them to his home for a Christmas feast, afterwards accusing them of stealing a silver cup he said was missing. Innocent, the unhappy pair were incarcerated in a tiny cell before meeting their fate at the Appleby Sessions.

As Dorothy said, the walls of Calgarth were strong - one was 7ft 6 inches thick! And from then on two skulls haunted the Hall. Despite all attempts to rid the Hall of its unwelcome guests they always reappeared to the niche at the top of the stairs! Over the years Calgarth Hall continued to echo to ghostly groans and screams.

The other part of the curse certainly worked, for an end did come to the Philipson's prosperity. It's odd that up to 1634 they acquired many acres of land, but after then the family suffered and the estates became impoverished by fines and the loss of property seized by Cromwell's parliament, the price the Philipsons paid for their loyalty to the Stuart throne.

The family died out and in 1777 Calgarth Hall was owned by William Penny, of Penny Bridge Hall, before going to the heirs of Myles Sandys, of Graythwaite. They sold it to Dr Richard Watson, the Bishop of Landaff, who exorcised the skulls and had them bricked up.

There were to be no more hauntings.

In 1880, local historian Dr Alexander Craig Gibson penned a verse that mentioned the skulls.

> To Calgarth Hall, in the midnight cold,
> Two headless skeletons cross the fold,
> Undid the bars, unlatched the door,
> And over the step passed down the floor,
> Where the jolly round porter sat sleeping.
> With a patter their feet on the pavement fall,
> And traverse the stairs that window's wall,
> Where out of a niche, at the witch hour dark,
> Each lifts a skull, all grinning and stark,
> And fits one on with a creaking,
> Then forth they go with a ghostly march,
> And bending low at the portal arch,
> Through Calgarth's woods, o'er Rydal Braes,
> And over the pass by Dunmail Raise,
> The two the course are keeping.

If the tale was true Myles Philipson was in no great need of the land owned by the Cooks. The Philipsons, who had lived at Calgarth Hall since 1332, were huge landowners. Myles, born in 1542, was the fifth and youngest son of Christopher Philipson, and his wife Elizabeth, (nee Briggs) and from his father inherited nearby Crook, lands at Cowperthwaite, a tenement called Tarn Close, the island on Lake Windermere and a tenement at Lyndeth.

Myles, who married Barbara, one of two daughters of William Sandys, of Conishead, was, on May 18, 1581, granted a Coat of Arms by Clarenceau, King of Arms.

Old Kendal records show that "under Applethwaite" Myles Philipson also owned a tenement and three acres. Could this have been that small plot once owned by Dorothy and Krasker Cook?

But then, on January 26, 1589, he granted to one James Wilson, an alderman, a parcel of ground, part of the grounds of Abbot Hall, together with a house standing there, to provide a Free School "for Godly and virtuous education, instruction and institution of youth of the said town and parish of Kirkby Kendal in Grammar and other good learning".

Was the silver cup tale a myth? Or was his later generosity simply a salve for a guilty conscience prompted by the haunting of the skulls?

The Hangman of Brigham

The dank November air hung shroud-like over the graveyard hard by St Bridget's Church in the West Cumberland village of Brigham.

It was 1757. The vicar, the Reverend Joseph Dixon, at the edge of an open grave and coming to the end of the burial service, intoned: "May God have mercy on his soul". They were words that the late Joseph Wilson would have heard many times when, as a hangman, he had assisted the condemned into the next world, words that were intoned by chaplains as those under sentence of death stood quaking, noose around neck, white hoods pulled over heads blocking out their last sight of this earthly world as they were about to be left dangling from the gibbet.

In Brigham's churchyard, making their last farewell to hangman Wilson would have been the family mourners. And there would have been quite a few "Amens" by the graveside, for the Wilson family had long resided in Brigham. Joseph was a family name, and he may well have been the Joseph Wilson whose son, also Joseph, was christened on December 5, 1697.

The Wilson interred on November 11 was listed in the Parish Register as: "Joseph Wilson, the common hangman of Eaglesfield". As Assizes cases punishable by death were always held in county towns and cities, he would have been the hangman at Carlisle.

Whether or not God did have mercy on his soul is debateable.

Legend has it that, sickened by his chosen calling - he would have been called on to hang many for what today are regarded as petty crimes - he died by his own hand, throwing himself off the Cocker Bridge and into the icy waters below, leaving his ghost to haunt St Bridget's churchyard for years to come.

Joseph Wilson's personal torment that led to his suicide may have been a result of his having to execute many an undeserving soul forced into crime by hunger and abject poverty. During the reign of George II death was the punishment not only for murder and rape, but for almost 200 crimes, including sheep stealing and poaching; the theft of a shilling incurred the death penalty. Forgery would also send you to the gallows, as would setting fire to a heap of hay or stealing a handkerchief worth more than one shilling.

St Bridget's, with its earliest nave and chancel dating back to 1090 - the nave was restored in 1865, the chancel in 1876 - was an important church in the later Middle Ages, serving Brigham - the "Homestead By The Bridge" - a parish of some 39,000 acres.

And there could been other spirits wandering abroad - those of the Vikings. There are six Viking Cross fragments in the church and a Cross base in the tower. A year book of the Cumberland and Westmoreland Archaeological and Antiquarian Society records: "Vikings rather liked being buried in Christian graveyards - before as well as after their conversion."

In 1814, a broadsword, two feet four inches long, its guard ornamented with inlaid silver, was discovered, along with a human skeleton, in a field at Eaglesfield owned by a Joseph Kendal. With the bones were an eleven-inch long halberd and a five-inch long fibula - a brooch used to fasten loose clothing.

Whether or not there was once the spirit of a tortured hangman, or even those of Vikings of days long gone, seeking their Valhalla - I found the old graveyard one of peace on the day I visited.

Close by the church door the neat and tidy monument to the soldiers of Brigham who died in two world wars stood gleaming in the midday sun; in the shade of nearby yew trees rank upon rank of ancient and ivy-grown slabs marked the resting places of the yeomen of yore.

When hangman Wilson was interred, his grave was marked by a tombstone that featured the main tool of his trade - it was edged with carvings depicting the rope. Over the years souvenir hunters picked away at it until none was left.

Perhaps that is why his ghost, with his last rope, the emblem of his macabre chosen calling, stolen, drifted away, never to haunt the ancient yard again!

Corby Castle

Guests for Henry Howard's house party at Corby Castle, standing high on the east bank of the River Eden, had been arriving from all over Cumberland during the previous afternoon and evening.

Henry had been born at the castle on July 2, 1757. After eight years of schooling in Paris, Vienna and Strasbourg - Catholics were obliged to seek education abroad - he came back to England to spend five years in the West Yorks Militia and eventually returned to Corby Castle, and his friends, in 1800.

Now it was September 8, 1803, and he was hosting one of the many weekend parties. His guests were to stay in his ancient home for some days. On the first morning the company had gathered around the breakfast table. Outside, the autumn sun rose to bring a sparkle to the velvet green lawns that swept up to the castle from the lodge house - just up the road from the village of Great Corby. The conversation was lively - Henry Howard's guests came from all walks of life - but the chatter suddenly stilled as a coach and four dashed up to the house in such haste that it knocked down part of the flower garden fence.

One couple at the table had been strangely silent. The man, Dr Henry Askew, Rector of Greystoke, stood up and declared: "It is our carriage. I am very sorry but we must absolutely leave you this morning."

If the other guests looked puzzled it was because they would not have known the circumstances and events that had forced the good reverend and his wife - the former Miss Anne Sutherland whom he had wed at Ulverston in July, 1799 - to so suddenly leave them.

The couple knew only too well.

THEY HAD SPENT A NIGHT OF TERROR IN A HAUNTED ROOM.

Their bedroom had not been one that was particularly remote or solitary. Far from it, it was surrounded on all sides by other rooms constantly in use. It was reached by a passage cut through a wall eight feet thick, and measuring 21ft by 18 ft. One side of the wainscoting was covered by tapestry, the remainder was covered with old family portraits, with, here and there, some ancient pieces of embroidery thought to be the work of nuns.

Pictures that hung in the castle were painted by Da Vinci, Titian, Corregio and Poussin. One of the treasures of Corby was the rosary of embossed gold beads and gold pendant cross worn round the waist by the tragic Mary, Queen of Scots, on her way to the scaffold. History was all around the reverend and his lady.

Over a cupboard that had doors of Venetian glass was an ancient oaken figure holding a battle axe, one of those placed on the walls on nearby Carlisle to represent guards. Hardly the sort of company to make you sleep easy in your bed in the hours of darkness. Imagine waking and seeing it looming over you like a vengeful knight, illuminated by the moon or - worse still - a flash of lightning.

Henry Howard's second wife, Catherine - Maria, his first wife had tragically died in childbirth just a year after their marriage - later told how she had tried to brighten up the bedchamber that struck fear into the hearts of those who slept there.

"There was an old fashioned bed and some dark furniture, but so many who slept here complained that I replaced these with more modern furniture," she said. "I hoped to remove that air of gloom which I thought might have given rise to the unaccountable reports of apparitions and extraordinary noises that were reaching us. I regret to say I did not succeed in banishing the nocturnal visitor who still continues to disturb our friends."

Catherine, the daughter of Sir Henry Neave, would have tried her best. Henry, her husband, said of her: She is my restorer to happiness who might well be taken as a model of judicious, careful and affectionate conduct as a wife and as a mother."

It was some six weeks later that Dr Askew, entertaining a party of some 20 people, among whom were some who previously had been total disbelievers in ghosts and hauntings, revealed the details of his night of horror at Corby.

"Soon after we went to bed we fell asleep," said the rector. "It might have been one and two in the morning when I awoke. I observed that the fire was totally extinguished, but although that was the case, and we had no light, I saw a glimmer in the centre of the room which suddenly increased to a bright flame. I looked out, apprehending that something had caught fire when, to my amazement, I beheld a beautiful boy, clothed in white, with bright locks resembling gold, standing by my bedside in which position he remained some minutes, fixing his eyes upon me with a mild and benevolent expression. He then glided towards the side of the chimney, where it is obvious there is no egress, and entirely disappeared. I found myself again in the total darkness and all remained quiet until the usual hour of rising."

Years later a Mrs Crowe produced a book of ghost stories - "Night Side of Nature" - in which she told how she was acquainted with some of the family and several friends of the Reverend Askew. She said: "He is now an old man, and I can positively assert that his own conviction with regard to the nature of the appearance has remained ever since unshaken. The circumstances made a lasting impression on his mind, and he never willingly speaks of it. When he does it is always with the greatest seriousness."

Historian Dr Henry Lonsdale said of Henry Howard: "His home was all that a man could wish for. Hosts of attached friends gathered under his rooftree. In his hands Corby Castle lost nothing of its ancient repute for profusely liberal hospitality, elegant society, and all the pleasant amenities of life."

But then, Lonsdale had no way of knowing about the elegant ghost that was definitely not one of the pleasant amenities of life at the castle.

Legend has it that whoever saw the boy would "first rise to the summit of power but then die by his own hand". The Reverend Henry Askew suffered no such fate. He remained a simple country rector until 1850, during which time he paid for the restoration of a thirteenth century window in his church which once had as a rector, in 1357, Richard De Hoton Roof. The reverend died in his bed of old age.

Workington Hall

The small boat, leaving behind the choppy waters of the Solway, wallowed its way past the breakwater, dropped sail and nudged into Workington harbour. Its original destination, as it set out from the little port at the mouth of the Abbey Burn on the other side of the estuary, had been France, but winds and tides had driven it off course.

The little vessel, more used to shipping lime and coal, came alongside the jetty where a man stepped ashore to then hand a regal, cloak-wrapped figure onto the quayside. He was Sir John Maxwell, a man educated at Sweetheart Abbey and created Lord Herries just two years before. The lady, with her red hair cropped short for disguise and concealed by a hood, was Mary, Queen of Scots. Following her ashore were sixteen ladies of her court. Mary Stuart was to spend her first night in England in Workington Hall.

It was 7 pm on the evening of Sunday, May 16, 1568, and the start of nineteen years of confinement for Mary, ended only, on the

orders of Queen Elizabeth I, by her execution at Fotheringhay Castle in Northamptonshire.

    If ever a ghost was to haunt Workington Hall surely it must have been that of the tragic Mary.

But it was the ghost of a later Sir Henry Curwen who was to disturb the sleep of those who were, in future years, to stay at the ancient home of the Curwens, the Cumbrian family that could trace its lineage back to at least the thirteenth century and the days of Edward I.

What Mary did leave behind was a small cup, made from Scottish agate, brought by Lord Herries from Dundrennan Abbey in the hastily packed basket of provisions for the journey. She gave it to Sir Henry and his wife Catherine, daughter of Sir John Dalston, saying "Luck to Workington". The Luck of Workington can, to this day, be seen at Belle Isle, Windermere. It was a gift in gratitude for his hospitality - there were to be no hauntings by the Queen of Scots.

Workington Hall was a building of some splendour. A massive mahogany door - like all the doors in the Hall made from timber from ships wrecked on the Cumbrian coast - guarded the Great Hall, seven foot thick walls formed the defensive Pele Tower. It was an imposing building that took on a grim air when, in the darkness of night, the ancient house echoed to a strange noise of bumping down the stairs.

Legend had it that it was the ghost of Sir Henry, known as Galloping Harry. It was a nick-name well earned. He owned a splendid horse called White Barb for which he had paid 300 guineas. The horse's progeny was in great demand by cavalry officers, and Sir Henry was ever ready to go galloping off on raids that took him north of the Border. He was one of the army that gathered in Carlisle when Thomas Radcliffe, Earl of Sussex, and Lord Scrope, Warden of the Western Marches, raided Scotland in 1570. Seven days later they returned, Galloping Harry boasting that they "had not left a stone house standing capable of giving shelter to armed men". He also brought back a trophy, the iron gate from Caerlaverock Castle that hung at Workington Hall for centuries.

Sadly, during the 1698 revolution, all of Galloping Harry's horses were seized after he was suspected of being a Papist.

In 1899 a later member of the family, John F. Curwen, told

the tale of the things that went bump in the night. "It seems that when Galloping Harry was nigh unto death, a French lady and her maid took him by the heels and pulled the old man down the stairs to a lower room where they seated him in a high-backed chair.

"Telling the servants that their master was much better and not to be disturbed, they immediately decamped with all the available jewellery and embarked in a small vessel from the harbour."

The ghostly disturbance at the Hall was the sound of Galloping Harry's head bumping down the stairs!

John Curwen went on: "Fifty years later an old woman appeared in Workington and reported that she had been the maid, that their vessel had sunk off the Scilly Isles, her mistress drowned, the valuables lost, and that she herself, having been saved by a French fishing smack, had taken the veil to find peace in a convent and had now come back to unburden her soul and die."

But there were others who claimed that the real reason Sir Henry, a devout Catholic, haunted the Hall was because his portrait had been turned to face the wall. It had been turned, they said, when the family changed faith, a Miss Curwen marrying Thomas Fairfax,

Oliver Cromwell's civil war general. This was nonsense. Fairfax did marry, but no Curwen. In 1637 he wed Anne Vere, daughter of his old commander, Sir Horace Vere. She died in 1665, Fairfax in 1671. They lie buried together in the churchyard at Bilborough, near York.

But more ghostly goings on were authenticated by an impeccable witness, and they were reported in the Workington Times &

Star in the nineteen fifties

The tale was set in the 'twenties, when Isabel, the last of the Curwens was living at the Hall. Said John Curwen: "There had been a shooting party in the High Woods, and the privileged few who had taken part were enjoying a drink in the library. Amongst them was Patricius Lamplugh Curwen, the Rector of Workington.

"On the rug before the great fire lay a couple of spaniels which had been doing their work during the day's shoot. The conversation flagged a little, then suddenly the two dogs rose to their feet and stared at the door in the corner of the room. The door was almost a secret one, cutting into one of the great library pictures, and it opened slowly.

THE HUMAN OCCUPANTS OF THE ROOM SAW NOTHING, BUT THE DOGS HAD THEIR EYES ON SOMETHING WHICH MOVED FROM THE DOOR TO A VACANT CHAIR BY THE FIRESIDE.

Then, for a while, they remained with their eyes fixed on the chair. The dogs then shifted their gaze as what they were seeing moved slowly back to the door which then closed and things returned - as nearly as they could in the circumstances - to normal."

It was a sensation experienced by several visitors to the Hall.

There was no reason to doubt the tale. It was told by the most impeccable of witnesses - the Reverend Canon Curwen himself.

And John Curwen added: "He was not joking!"

24

Gill House

That Gill House was once haunted is indisputable. Over the years credible witnesses have almost queued up to attest to the authenticity of tales of knocks in the night, faces at windows, footsteps heard where feet were never seen, and, horror of horrors, the smell of putrefying flesh.

The intriguing question is: "The ghost of whom?"

Was it the Satanist Gerald Reay, the sacrilegious monster who stole the Host - the consecrated bread - from St Kentigern's Church?

Was it his grandson, Jackson Reay, who murdered his wife Elisabeth but was found insane?

Who was the ghostly figure so often seen dragging a long haired girl through the churchyard at nearby Bromfield, the village that lies just off the Wigton-Aspatria road?

And who was the little girl in Victorian dress who appeared at an upstairs window only to have the shutters slammed shut by the man in black behind her?

Reports of strange happenings at the house - originally dating back to the 1200s and always in the possession of the Reay family - first came to light in 1943. The first three nights of the wane of the moon had become nights of terror at Gill House, then a hostel for the Women's Land Army, the volunteer force working in agriculture in World War II years.

The girls, in light brown overalls for work, and with a smart off-duty uniform of stout brown shoes, green jumpers, corduroy jodphurs and board-brimmed khaki hat, tackled many tasks. They were potato planting at Armathwaite, stooking sheaves at Rockliffe. Others were snagging turnips and muck-spreading. They could look on with pride at St Kentigern's Harvest Festival service.

But for some of them there was no rest at the end of hardworking days. Their bedroom was haunted.

The then national newspaper The Daily Dispatch spooked their readers with the tale, reporting: "One night last week the whole dormitory was thrown into panic by the screams of one girl who declared she had suddenly awakened with the feeling she was being strangled and pulled through the bed."

One person who knew most about the haunting of Gill House was Mrs Helen Parkin, an East Cumbria Land Army administration officer, who volunteered to investigate after West Cumbria officials declined. Assisting Mrs Parkin was to be the vicar of Ainstable, the Reverend Norman Murray and his wife.

On July 17, 1943, County Organiser Mrs Soulsby, based at HQ in Penrith, telephoned Mrs Parkin. Feeling was running high at the hostel - she thought it possible that the girls would walk out. Would Mrs Parkin go to Gill House that night?

At 10 pm Mrs Parkin left her Broomrigg home, collected the Murrays, and arrived at the hostel at 11.45 pm. The hauntings always happened between 12 pm and 3 am.

Her report proved that the Land Army girls had not exaggerated. Nor were the strange happenings, as some thought, the work of village lads playing tricks.

The trio entered the haunted room at 11.55 pm, the vicar and

Mrs Murray were on the window seat. Mrs Parkin, who sat at the foot of one of the five beds in the room, then recorded: "Mr Murray said that one could often start these things by knocking. He told me to knock the cupboard door. I did so, and though there were only two Land Army greatcoats hanging up and one pair of Wellington boots in the cupboard my knock was answered by a noise like the rustling of tissue paper if you rubbed it together - and out he came!

"THE FOOTSTEPS WERE LOUD AND CLEAR AND CAME STRAIGHT THROUGH THE HEAD OF THE BED ON WHICH I WAS SITTING. He came right round the bed and stood next to me...

"He stood right next to me and there was a loud noise right at my ear. I likened the noise to the quick winding of a reel as you play a fish. The Murrays both heard the noise, and Mr Murray likened

it to the winding of a large clock.

"Then all the warmth was taken out of me and though it was a hot night I was frozen.

"He then left me and went to Mr Murray and started to tap on the wall, then went tapping all the way to the fireplace. Mr Murray got up and followed him. Then he came back, still tapping at the wall. It was a sort of metallic sound, as though he was tapping with a penny. Then we all got a wave of the most filthy smell. On the way home Mr Murray said he had experienced the same dreadful smell once before, when he was a curate taking a funeral and the coffin leaked."

The ghost, nick-named Christopher by the girls, tapped on until 3 am.

Later the vicar told Mrs Parkin that ghosts manifest themselves by using surplus energy, and as young people give out more energy than older people the whole hostel had become a storage battery of energy given out by the girls living there.

The next morning Mrs Parkin phoned Mrs Soulsby, the County Organiser, and told her what had happened, later that day posting to her a written report. In the afternoon the Murrays arrived at her home with a planchette - a heart-shaped board on small wheels holding a pencil and said to receive messages from spirits when a hand is held over it.

Said Mrs Parkin: "I cannot make one move myself, but the strange part was that without me the Murrays could not get anything about Gill. Mr Murray was so psychic that if he held his hand eighteen inches over the planchette it worked."

Mrs Parkin's report then detailed a question and answer session using the board. MR M, obviously, was the vicar, his wife Mrs M; the letter P was the spirit guide's answer.

Mr M: Who are we speaking to?

P: Kettle. Power comes from Ossery, Kilkenny.

Mr M: Can you tell us anything about Gill?

P: WLA hostel.

Mr M: Is it haunted?

P: Yes.

Mr M: Who by?

P: Gerald Reay.

Mr M: Did he commit a murder?

P: No.

Mr M: Then why does he haunt it?

P: Hostea incarceri fecit.

Mr M: Please translate that

P: Gerald stole the Host.

After a few more questions the vicar asked: "Why did Gerald steal the Host?"

P: To practise sorcery. Gerald practices the Adam Rites.

Mr M: Does anybody else haunt the Gill?

P: Yes. Lily. Gerald called her "My Lily".

Mrs M: Who was Lily?

P: Bastard servant.

A little later the vicar asked: "Did Gerald kill Lily?"

P: No. Lily died of consumption, aged 24, and is buried in the garden.

Mr M: When did Gerald die?

P: Gerald died aged 54 and was buried in Bromfield churchyard.

Not one of the investigating trio thought that such a burial seemed strange considering the theft of the Host and the sorcery!

The vicar carried on: What was that terrible smell at Gill.

P: Lily's body.

At this point in a later report Mrs Parkin noted that the entity called Kettle left and that was all they could get that day. She added: "Canon Pythian Adams, of Carlisle Cathedral, was very interested in the haunting, and traced Kettle. She was a nun living in the 1200's in a convent in Ossery, Kilkenny."

The Canon was no amateur investigator. He had worked with Harry Price, the man who investigated Borley Rectory, Britain's most haunted building. Later, writing in the Church Quarterly Review, he said: "My own impression, after studying the evidence, is that all poltergeist phenomena are of human origin, and that they are connected with the life (and death) history of the particular personality....

"We are none of us perhaps very far from those primeval pulsings of life which some call the devil and others the great god Pan."

A second session with the planchette took place on Thursday, July 22. Their spirit guide identified himself as William Olgivie, a Jacobite who came to Brampton with Bonnie Prince Charlie's army and who had been killed in a duel.

Mr M: Can you tell us how long Gill has been haunted?

P: We do not know time as you know it.

V: Can you tell us then which king was on the throne when Gerald stole the Host and the evil started?

P: George the Pretender.

Mr M: Can you tell us why the haunting takes place on the three nights before the wane of the moon?

At this point the planchette spelt out a jumble of letters making no sense. Mrs Parkin exclaimed: "This is nonsense!"

The planchette responded: It is not nonsense, it is Gaelic, get it translated.

Canon Pythian Adams later not only traced a William Olgivie. He confirmed he was a Jacobite and that he had been killed in a duel. The Canon also sent the jumbled message to Aberdeen University; the Reverend Murray sent a copy to Glasgow University. Both translated it as reading: "On these Holy nights cursed be he who hurts the man."

After the WLA London headquarters received the report of the haunting they sent a Mrs Howes to investigate.

She arrived at Gill House on the first night of the wane of the moon; with the warden, Miss Mandale; she planned to spend a night in the haunted room.

The Daily Dispatch gleefully reported: "Before dawn broke both had left the dormitory, pale and haggard."

Miss Mandale told Mrs Parkin: "At 11.55 pm Mrs Howes and I went into the haunted room and lay on the two beds either side

of the fireplace. Just after midnight the footsteps came out from the cupboard and came straight to me. There was a loud noise, like the sharpening of shears, and I felt my hair being touched. I called out: 'Please don't cut my hair off!' It left me and went to Mrs Howes. It then lifted the wire mattress from under her and pulled the pillow from under her head. We both jumped out of bed and fled!"

Mrs Howes later told a friend: "I had three hair-raising experiences which nearly reduced me to a state of panic."

After this the building was abandoned, the girls were moved to other hostels before the month was out.

But for Mrs Parkin there were to be more strange discoveries. She told how one of her land girls was to marry a local lad and had come to her house to discuss the possibility of a job in Kirklinton, where her fiance was working. Later the girl said: "It was you who went to Gill, Mrs Parkin."

She agreed. The girl's fiance then said: "When I was a lad I was hired on a farm near Gill. We lads would cycle four or five miles out of our way to get to Bromfield because when the moon was bright the figure of a man had been seen many times pulling a young girl by the hair along the road from Gill to Bromfield churchyard."

Further sightings of the spectral pair came from another reliable source. In July, 1945, the Reverend Murray left Ainstable to take up the living of Eaglesfield, near Cockermouth. On arrival a lady

churchwarden told him that his new vicarage was haunted. The vicar then told her about Gill. He was astonished to hear that when she and her brother were children they lived in a farmhouse in Bromfield, which backed onto the churchyard. She told him: "Many a time we saw a man pulling a girl by the hair through the churchyard and up to the Reay family tomb!"

In 1943, Mary Heddon - coincidentally the mother of Lena Askew, one of the Land Army Girls - was walking with her husband, her son, and a friend, and were passing Gill House which they knew was then empty. They had a look around, and before leaving, turned for a last look. Said Mrs Heddon: "All four of us saw a little girl in white with long golden hair standing in an upstairs window. Then there came from behind her a man or a woman, I'd say a man as it was a tall, well-built person in what appeared top be a black suit. He put out both his arms, one each side of the girl, and closed the shutters."

Lena can recall those days of the summer of 1943. As she sat in her home now in Carlisle's Blackwell Place, she told me: "I was one of those who refused to sleep in the haunted room. It was my mother, Mary Heddon, then living at Langrigg, who saw the man in black slam the shutters in front of the little girl."

Lena told how they worked at many farms in the area, all for four pounds a week with half of that stopped to pay for their keep.

"We went muckspreading at Abbeytown. We snagged turnips, and stood on rat-infested stacks at threshing time. They did say they would teach me how to drive a tractor. They did. But they didn't show me how to stop it! I did so by driving into a tree."

Lena recalled another strange sighting: "Elsie Dargie, a friend who lived in the nearby village of Langrigg, told me how she had once stood in front of Gill House and looked through one of the French windows." Elsie said: "I saw a girl, about ten or twelve years old, long golden hair, a sailor collar and white stockings. She ran across the room to the stairs. Some years later I saw a man sitting in the same room. It was a Sunday. He sat with a book or a paper on his lap. He had long black hair, a lovely face and had on a rough, sacking-like, dressing gown. He was very close to me. I seemed to blink

and he had gone. The room was bare."

The day that the Land Army girls left Gill a medium from Chester, who had read of the hauntings in a newspaper, arrived. Miss Mandale, the only person left, was packing crockery in the kitchen. She was too busy to stay with the medium but did take her up to the room.

A little later she came down to announce; "You have not only one ghost, there are two - a very vivid man in early Georgian clothes and a mere wraith of a girl with long fair hair."

The Land Army may well have abandoned the haunted hostel but the ghosts were still there. Were they Gerald and the unfortunate Lily? Were they Jackson Reay and his wife Elisabeth? The Carlisle Journal of September 16, 1810, reported the trial of Jackson. He was found guilty of murdering Elisabeth, but insane. The Assize judge had heard how he had battered her to death with an iron wedge as she lay in bed with her two young children. The court had heard that if there was a knock at the door Jackson would flee in terror, claiming that the Devil was after him.

In later years Gill was used as a Preparatory School. At that time Margaret worked there as a maid. Later she was to tell Mrs Amy Sidaway, who, with her husband Nigel, has lived there for over thirty years: "I used to work for Mr Campbell, the headmaster. I was doing holiday work and alone in the school when I saw an apparition coming down the stairs, through the hall and out of the door. I followed! But not before leaving a note that read: 'I've seen the ghosts. I'm not coming back again, ever!'"

In 1944 Dom Richard Wright, the Roman Catholic priest at Warwick Bridge, came to dinner with Mrs Parkin. He told her that often at Mass he had a strange feeling that he must pray to the Sacred Heart where Gill was concerned. On March 10, the Feast of St Joseph, Father Wright said a Mass of Reparation at Warwick Bridge.

It seemed to have worked. Gill House is now ghost free. It is warm and welcoming. A curved staircase that winds under what was the haunted room leading up to a long gallery. Ornate and beautiful Italian plasterwork - said to be that of the artisans who worked on Lowther castle - decorates the high ceilings. Outside gardens run down to the stream that gurgles along the gill from which the house takes its name.

I had knocked on the cupboard door. I had heard no footsteps, nor sounds of rustling paper.

The lovely old house is at peace with itself.

Hutton Hall's Headless Lady

Countrymen returning home after a day out and a drink or two in Penrith would claim that they had the eeriest of experiences when passing the old Toll Bar near Hutton Hall (now known as Hutton in the Forest), the thirteenth century stronghold that was home to Adam De Hoton, who died there in 1308. Some would return to their families white faced and trembling with fear to tell how their horses had shied and snorted, breaking into a mad gallop as they neared what legend said was a haunted spot.

Some even claimed to have seen a low carriage drawn by two white ponies driven by a headless woman in white.

"I heard the clatter of horses' feet and the rattle of carriage wheels on the road we call Kelbar Lonning," said a woman known as Janet, who first saw the apparition and was also alleged by author Ian Davidson to be the mother of the knight of Hutton Hall's illegitimate son, Davie.

Davidson first told the story in his book The Ghost of Hutton Hall published in 1932. He told how, on wintry nights, the old men of those parts, warming themselves at a smithy fire, would sit and tell the tales of legend.

Davidson first heard of Hutton's ghost from a man who had a strange experience on the spot where the old toll bar stood. With him was a sheepdog called Sharrow - they had been out moving a flock - who refused to pass the spot and kept tugging his master away. It was this man's great grandfather, Thomas, who had recalled the dreadful day when he had been courting his girl, Mary, at nearby Ellonby and was returning home late.

"A sudden shriek startled me he said, And then I saw two white ponies dash through the overgrown gateway to the park drive, dragging after them the low carriage and, most awful horror of all, there, seated bolt upright in the vehicle, was the headless body of the lady, the wife of the Knight of Hutton Hall. I can see it all as clearly now as I saw it then and remember how she was dressed in white, and the reins were so placed that she appeared to be actually holding them and driving.

"The ponies tore past me at fearful rate, ears laid back, necks outstretched, nostrils extended and snorting; pressing together in a frenzied gallop, as if under the power of some evil spirit. So rapid

was their pace that the carriage bounced and swayed from one side of the road to the other, but still the gruesome figure in the carriage maintained its upright position. A sight more awesome, more appalling, more terrifying it would be impossible to imagine.

"The maddened ponies very soon carried the dreadful load out of sight, but for some time I could hear their hooves clattering on the highway. The poor frightened creatures were evidently making for the hall. I was too terror stricken to move or cry out. I must have reeled and fallen in a swoon and lain there in the roadway for some considerable time, for when I began to gather my senses it was long past midnight and a silence prevailed which only emphasised the horror that began to slowly come back to my bewildered brain.

"With a cry of utter terror I fled along the road in the opposite direction to that taken by the frightful vision I had seen. I have no very clear recollection of reaching home, but I must have arrived there, for the next thing I remember was my mother bending over me with a cup of something to drink and I call to mind how she said, as I opened my eyes, 'Thank God he's better.'

"I was told afterwards that I had rushed into the house, for the door was open as they had been watching for me, and fallen exhausted on the settle in the kitchen, unable to speak a word in the way of explanation. They then carried me up to bed where I lay for three days in a fever of delirium, babbling all the time of something no one could understand."

Legend has it that, some years earlier, there had been a great commotion and the wildest rumours about the disappearance of a lady of Hutton Hall. It was her personal maid who first discovered that there was something wrong. Going into her mistress' room she found the bed not used, nor was there any sign of her or any evidence of her presence anywhere in the hall or the grounds. So far as the maid could discover, her mistress had been wearing her white summer walking costume, and the wardrobe was undisturbed.

Almost immediately after her discovery the groom, in a great state of agitation, came in from the stables to report that the ponies were missing and so was the carriage. But the most startling piece of news was yet to come. A little later the knight was found dead. His body lay a few yards away from the outhouse, face downward as if he had been about to leave the building and had fallen forward. In his hand was his heavy walking stick, which he always carried.

A doctor certified that death was due to heart failure, probably brought on by a great shock. He had a weak heart and had been warned not to become excited. Rumour associated the shock with finding the ponies and carriage missing and believing that his wife, who often was seen walking alone in the nearby woods, had run off with a lover.

But what had become of her? The woods and grounds were searched but no trace could be found.

How the countryside would have gossiped. Joseph Capstick, mine host of the nearby Clickham Arms would have heard the tale; so, too, would the patients of Dr MacGregor, chattering away in his Kirkoswald surgery.

A wandering Cumbrian musician, Fiddler Willie, often told how the lady's pet dog had been seen wandering restlessly through the hall and grounds, sometimes lying whining on the bank at the

41

edge of the lake, his head between his paws. When brought away he would keep looking back at the lake. Later he was found drowned there.

Legend has it that the lady's body rests in that lake. And that when it was drained to allow cleansing and deepening work, embedded in the mud at the bottom were the remains of a carriage and harness.

It was a gloomy late November day when I was on the road that skirts Hutton Hall. I stood on the spot where once there was a toll bar or turnpike. It is shown on a 1770 map, just where a lane leads off to Kellgarrow. Behind me a signpost pointed to Kellgarrow Farm but the only shiver I got was caused by the cold wind and rain.

Just up the road, past the grey granite houses adorned with the V - for Vane - is what was once a wide entrance to the grounds of Hutton Hall. Now unused, it is grassy with a sprinkling of weeds. But the ornate railings still stand each side of a space that would allow easy passage for a carriage and horses.

There was a lake. That, too, is shown on the old map. On that wet day when I passed by a deep stream still gurgled through the grounds.

Hutton Hall was the home of a knight. But from here on the facts appear to stray from the legend.

Hutton in the Forest was bought in 1606 by Richard Fletcher, High Sheriff of Cumberland. His son Henry was created baronet in 1645, but this Sir H died for the Royalist cause at the Battle of Rowton Heath. Janet, the mother of illegitimate Davie, first saw the apparition at the time that Border Reivers were attacking Netherby so this first sighting could have happened in the mid 1600's.

There was a later Sir H - Henry, son of Sir George Fletcher who was Mayor of Carlisle in 1671. This Sir Henry changed religion to become a Roman Catholic and retired to live in the Monastery at Douai. He never married, and neither could I find any record of a knight of Hutton dying on the day that his wife disappeared.

The raconteur in Davidson's book has it that the lady was

murdered by a wandering thief named Harland who allegedly stabbed her and then cut off her head. He had talked a young man, Alan Irving, son of Alan Irving and his wife Elspeth, who lived at Woodend and was once employed at Hutton, but sacked for "presumptuous familiarity" when addressing the Lady of the Hall, into breaking into the stables and bringing round the ponies and carriage to the toll bar site to dispose of the body.

Was there an awful apparition that reran the events of that night of horror - or were the spirits conjured up by other spirits? Those sold in the inns and taverns of Penrith perhaps?

Carlisle Journal Ghost

If ever a building was to be haunted it was surely the one that one stood in English Street. In its past it had been a proud four-storied edifice reigning over that end of Carlisle's main street in which stood the statue of James Steel, one-time Mayor of the city and one-time editor and proprietor of the Carlisle Journal.

I first saw it in the 'fifties. By then it had acquired an air of shabby gentility, the Journal's golden days as the city's premier newspaper - founded in 1798 and seventeen years before the Carlisle Patriot - were long gone.

Throughout the rambling building there were echoing spaces where once journalistic giants of the past had reported the daily doings of Cumberland.

But the earlier top-hatted writers had passed into history. In more recent timers Teddy Trow had left to join the Daily Mail as agricultural correspondent, Rodney Hallworth was now the Mail's crime writer; Cyril Ainsley had said farewell to English Street to become chief reporter of the Daily Express.

Old battle-horse Ernest Williams, of indeterminate age but possibly in his eighties, once news editor of the Cumberland News but sacked for a disgraceful headline (Farewell Sir Fergus the Futile!) when Sir Fergus Graham lost his seat as the city's Member of Parliament, the silver-haired doyen of Carlisle journalists, occupied a glassed windowed cubby-hole. I was then a cameraman. One day, testing a flashgun in the room next door brought a shriek of anguish from Ernest. His quiff quivering, he cried: "My God! Lightning without thunder. It's dangerous!" We did not enlighten him!

Ernest was always conscious of the social niceties. He told me: "You must always remember to address the Bishop as 'My Lord'." I was with him on one occasion when he did address the Bishop. I swear that as well as the 'My Lord' he bowed and touched his silver forelock!

Each morning, as he arrived he removed his detachable shirt-collar. Before leaving I would be summoned to help him replace it. Then, before leaving to catch the bus to Talkin village, where he lived with his daughter and on Fridays ruled the back room of the Hare and Hounds, he would spin round three times - it was a superstition unknown to the rest of us.

He was equally well known to the drivers and conductresses of the Ribble bus service. Seconds before the morning bus was due to leave a window would open and through it would pop Ernest's head. "You must wait for me!" he would cry. They always did! There were times that he wheedled the conductresses into tying his shoe-laces which he had overlooked in his rush for the bus.

The Journal's front windows bowed to the commercial. Envelopes, writing pads, shelf paper and loo rolls were on display. It was a side industry managed by Company Secretary F. Donald Ayers. Every penny was welcome!

When well-known author Hunter Davies was a student at Durham University he worked for the Journal during vacations. Waiting for him outside the loo-roll filled windows would be girl-friend Margaret Forster - later to become Hunter's wife and a famous novelist. Hunter to this day claims that I taught him his first lesson in journalism - how to fill in an expenses form!

To the side of the windows stood a door. Just inside was the iron staircase that spiralled upwards to the editorial offices. The huge room with a view over English Street was that of Editor Eric Scholey. He was later replaced by Fred Humphrey, a member of the National Liberal Club, who collected a wartime OBE serving with the Central Office of Information, and who, at a ripe old age, had fathered seven children by his second "wife", whilst rumour had it that his first (and proper?) wife hung around the annual conferences of the National Union of Journalists seeking what would appear to be a long-lost spouse!

The floor above had two rooms that contained the photo-engraving department and three rooms for editorial use. One provid-ed space for Sports Editor Bob Moore, the other for reporter Dick

Allen, women's page writer Gillian Haughan, and juniors Brian McGlone and Michael Rowe, the latter a lean and hungry genius who enthusiastically reported Cumberland and Westmoreland wrestling, who learned Russian solely to ensure he did his National Service in Military Intelligence and on a whim learned to play flamenco guitar. He was later to cross Russia on the Trans-Siberian railway, land in Japan with half a crown in his pocket and later walk with cousin Mickey Rowe over the Mountains of the Moon and through the Khyber Pass. His graphic dispatches from far distant lands made full-page features for the Journal. Sadly he died at a young age as editor of the Canadian paper The Trail Bugle.

The top floor had rooms with dormer windows, once for editorial use, but now home for a commercial photographic developing and printing operation.

It was a humble, but proud little paper. And it had moments when it scored over the mighty Cumberland News! We had our scoops. Dick Allen brought back the first news that Spadeadam was to be the testing ground for the Blue Streak rocket.

When tragic Ma Duckett was murdered in her small sweet shop in Carlisle's Tait Street Brian McGlone was first to connect the murder with John Wilson Vickers, arrested and held on a vague charge of stealing a car headlamp. Brian and I discovered the name of one of Ma Duckett's friends. She was returning from a day out in Blackpool. We picked her out from the crowd on Carlisle Station, got her a taxi to her Stanwix home and secured the only picture available of the victim.

Bob Moore covered Carlisle United. He was outspoken. He was once banned from travelling on the team coach. One of his more memorable headlines was: "They're calling me the gloomy Dean of soccer!"

To Ernest was delegated the covering of Rotary lunches and council meetings. Copy was scrawled with pen and ink. Dick Allen covered Assizes and Quarter Sessions held at the English Street Courts. Somewhere in the bound-files room a junior Brian or Michael would be digging out items for the 'news of 100 years ago' column.

But Ernest would lay down his pen and the clatter of the old 'sit-up-and-beg typewriters' would cease at 11 am. It was coffee time. Just across English Street was the Silver Grill, with its chauvinistic curtained off 'men only' area. We would troop across to sit in wickerwork chairs and swap gossip with our opposite numbers on the News and Star who also popped in.

At the rear of the building the ground floor held the old printing press, one of those on which, years before, the London Evening Standard had been printed. An open staircase led up to the caseroom with its typesetting machines and steel-topped tables on which pages were made up.

The back door led out to Blackfriars Street - in it, just a few yards across the road, the site of the old Blackfriars Monastery where skeletons lay just a few feet under the surface, just up the road a churchyard with a gruesome tale to tell.

What self-respecting ghost then could ignore such a happy haunting ground!

Twice I came to shivery close quarters with he, she or it. Reporter Sid Clarke, an upright Quaker who would never tell a lie, had an eerie experience on a landing at the top of the stairs that wound upwards through the separate floors.

It was a Thursday night when I first experienced the inexplicable. The Carlisle Journal was printed late evening on Thursdays. After the last page had gone to press some, in true journalistic tradition, would repair to The Sportsman Inn, conveniently situated at the corner of Heads Lane and Blackfriars Street, a few steps from the back door.

Back in the building Bob Moore and I were waiting to pick up a copy of the paper, hot off the press. It was about 9.30 pm, and we were whiling away the time playing cricket - for safety using a ball made of scrunched up paper bound with sellotape.

Then came the sound. It was no trick of the imagination. Three loud and distinct knocks on the door that once opened into the smaller room but now could not be opened because of a slight subsidence of the building.

Junior reporter Brian McGlone was a japer. Once, when ancient Ernest had been ill and not in the office, he had climbed the stairs that also passed the door of the editor's room, and, in a perfect imitation of Ernest's voice, wished us all "Good Morning". Days later a perplexed Fred Humphrey demanded to know from an even more perplexed Ernest just why he had been in the office when he was ostensibly ill, and why he had not reported to him!

After hearing the three knocks Bob and I had the same thought. It must be Brian! I was standing by the door that was open to the landing. It was the only way down, we agreed that I would guard it and Bob would search the other rooms.

THERE WAS NO-ONE ELSE ON THAT FLOOR.

No Brian up to his tricks. bob and I looked at each other. A shiver went down my back. Without a word we both fled to the ground floor - and the to The Sportsman!

The next morning we tried to recreate the noise. We dropped books off the shelf, we slammed the door in the small room. It was impossible.

We had heard three knocks - not gentle taps - on that door and no-one had been there!

Some months later I had been covering an event at the Crown and Mitre and it was past midnight as I entered the Journal building by the back door - in those days one could leave the Mitre by its back door and exit onto Blackfriars Street.

Deciding not to climb the three flights of stairs at the front of the ground floor I left my equipment by the printing press. As I did so I froze. Clearly I heard the sound of footsteps descending the open wooden staircase that led up to the caseroom. Each step set the stairs creaking. I had switched on the lights and the staircase was clearly illuminated.

The foot steps continued downwards. AGAIN THERE WAS NO-ONE THERE!

I fled, my fear not eased by having to struggle to open the exit door - it had a faulty knob! Seconds later - it seemed like minutes - a trembling Kemp stood outside, relishing the night-time peace of the lamp-lit Blackfriars Street.

It was the Quaker Sid Clarke who confirmed our suspicions that the building had a ghost. Confirmation came the day that Sid reached the landing outside the room where Bob and I heard the knocking.

On that summer's day he found himself engulfed in an atmosphere of icy-cold air. He admitted to feeling frightened and had no explanation. Bob and I knew. That building was haunted.

Later, when the building was being pulled down to make way for the new Littlewoods Store building, tough demolition workers told of being scared!

So who was the Journal ghost? Perhaps it was the lost soul of one of the Black Friars? When work started on the new Marks & Spencer food store excavations led to the discovery of many skeletons just yards away from where the Journal once stood.

Was it the spirit of a body that should have been at rest in the nearby St Cuthbert's churchyard? It was known that notorious grave robbers Burke and Hare had been active in the city, stealing cadavers for Dr Knox's medical research in Edinburgh.

In September, 1823, a young boy died after a coach accident, and was buried in St Cuthbert's. In December a body was discovered half dragged from its grave. The remains were those of a butcher who had died just weeks before. Investigation revealed two more missing bodies, one was that of the boy who died after the coach accident.

Whilst Macready's Theatre - opposite the graveyard - was staging "Virginius, or the Liberation of Rome" (with comic songs from Mr Lane from the Theatre Royals of York and Newcastle) more macabre activities across the road were liberating bodies of the newly dead! The Carlisle Journal of 1823 reported the ghastly affair:

·   "Monday evening, during the interrment of a corpse in St Cuthbert's churchyard a human body was discerned at a short distance, partly uncovered, which, on being raised up, was found to be the remains of a blacksmith who had been interred on the 11th Ult. It was perfectly naked, a cord tied round the feet which were drawn towards the head so that the body was almost bent double and altogether presented a a most disgusting and shocking spectacle."

The report continued: "During the last three days several graves have been opened by friends of the deceased; but the only bodies hitherto discovered to have been stolen are those of a boy, six years of age, named Lancaster, who died in consequence of having been overturned with a stagecoach for which he had a thigh amputated; and a cotton spinner of the name of Irving who was interred about three weeks since.

"It has been ascertained that a considerable number of packing boxes have been manufactured here for the express purpose of inclosing subjects for the school of anatomy at Edingburgh."

(The anatomy school was that of Dr John Knox - a one-time tutor and friend of Carlisle-born Dr Henry Lonsdale - whose lectures on anatomy and physiology unwittinglly, or so he claimed, used bodies provided by the notorious murderers Burke and Hare at £10 each.)

"A woman residing in the neighbourhood of Pattinson and Co's Brewery, close to Backhouse Walk, at a very untimely hour, perceived a man carrying a heavy package down the Sallyport, and soon after another man appeared similarly laden, and then a third; she could not, however, distinguish what sort of pacakages they were, but they appeared to be weighty."

Unhappy souls galore! Legend also had it that somebody committed suicide in the building, the body found hanging from a beam. But then again, perhaps the Journal's ghost was a result of the collective torment of those who had worked for the newspaper over the years.

Editors have been known to drive hard men almost to death!

Peggy Sneddle

The travellers gathered round the fire in The Elephant Inn shivered and pulled their cloaks a little closer. It was a chilling tale that Mine Host Dick Atkinson was telling.

"Aye. 'Twas in the days long back - when I was keeper of the tollgate on yon road that runs from Crackenthorpe to Appleby - that I was affeared whenever Helm Wind blew down from Cross Fell.

'Twould be then that a ghastly vision would set my legs a trembling. 'Twere that Mistress Machell in a carriage pulled by six horses, black as night, with long tails and flaming eyes and flaring nostrils, would come a-rushing out of the gate to Crackenthorpe Hall.

"There was a coachman a-wearing a three-cornered hat and huge jackboots. Behind them came other folk, all a-riding horses.

"Suddenly, with a wild blast, the tollgate was burst open and, with long unhallowed shrieks, the unearthly team, with the wan-faced apparition of Mistress Machell in the carriage, disappeared into the midnight darkness."

It was not for nothing that the locals called Cross Fell the Fiend's Fell. The wind, unique to the North Pennines, has been known as the Helm for over 1,000 years.

David Uttley, in his comprehensive book on the Helm Wind, said: "The local inhabitants have been aware of its baleful effects since antiquity; it is a cold, dry, violent wind from the East which desiccates and scorches all vegetation in its path..."

In the days when horses worked the fields they were made unsettled and bad-tempered by the wind that came screaming out of the hills at forty miles an hour. The noise wore people down; schoolchildren in class became restless.

If indeed there was a ghost with tantrums - no wonder!

It was a similar tale that local historian Lionel Cresswell, who in 1932 visited Crackenthorpe Hall with a party of antiquarians, came to tell.

"Country folk hereabouts tell of one Peg Sneddle who was no better than she should have been during life and still more troublesome after death. So much so that that when the river happened to be low they rolled aside a large boulder of Shap granite lying in the river bed a little below the Hall, dug a grave there, upended Peg from her resting place in consecrated ground and, after putting her into the new grave, rolled back the boulder.

"The accompanying exorcism was, I am told, performed by a Roman Catholic priest, the reason, I suppose, being that the Latin tongue is the one necessary to control disturbed and unquiet spirits. Since then she only walks only once a year. She has to be there for 999 years.

"The reputed portrait of Elisabeth Sleddall or Peg Sneddle - one or the other, or neither - hangs in the Central hall. A very buxom ghost!

"Her wraith is said to rise from the river once a year in September and find its way through the blocked up window of the King's Room at Crackenthorpe Hall.

"The countryfolk also say she has been seen to drive along the Appleby road at a great pace and with 'amber leets' in the carriage, to then disappear suddenly in Machell's Wood near the spot called Peg Sneddle's Trough.

"When the Helm Wind is blowing and storms raging on the Fell Peg is said to be in her tantrums and in more gracious mood in fine weather."

Historian Cresswell told how an old oak tree that once stood near Crackenthorpe was called Sleddall's Oak. A female figure, supposed to be that of Mistress Machell's ghost, was seen under it when any misfortune was to befall the Machell family. "Some times she is said to have appeared to the heads of the family when they were about to die."

So who was this Elizabeth Sleddall, alias Peg Sneddle, whose haunting ways scared the wits out of the good folk of the Eden Valley?

On November 13, 1643, at St Andrew's Church, Elizabeth, daughter of Penrith man Thomas Sleddall, married Lancelot Machell of Crackenthorpe Hall.

The Machells had lived in Cumberland since Norman times. Halth De Maechael and his wife Eve were mentioned in the Domesday Book - one of very few in the North-west corner of England. In 1332 William Mareschal was listed as one of fourteen local taxpayers. In 1423, after the death of Lord John Clifford, the Crackenthorpe estate passed to a John Machell.

Joseph Nicholson and Richard Burns's Directory of Cumberland, which they published in 1777, recorded: "The Machells seemed to have continued and resided at this place longer than any one family of note at any other place in the county.... Above the degree of yeoman always and seldom, or never, ascending to the degree of knight. Esquires and gentlemen constantly; and peculiarly remarkable in all generations for a brave and martial spirit."

William Dugdale, Norroy King of Arms, made one of his heraldic visitations to Westmorland in 1666 but once again failed to recognise the standing of the Machells.

Lancelot's second son Thomas, one-time Rector of Kirkby Thore, later Dean of Queen's College, Oxford and Chaplain in Ordinary to Charles II - also an antiquary - was scathing about Dugdale, saying: "He has entered for several generations squires who were never gentlemen and entered others as gentlemen only those who were most ancient squires, as the Machells of Crackenthorpe."

Indeed an old family, and David Balfour, who, with his wife Angela, now owns the Hall, tells how it may have descended from a Roman ancestor. He points out the two Roman altar stones that flank the Machell coat of arms inserted in the Hall's West wall, and records show a statement, written in Latin, in which a William Malus Catulus granted Crackenthorpe to his brother Alexander.

Brave and martial the Machells certainly were, and ever ready to support King Henry VI in the Wars of the Roses. Two Machells from Newbiggin were slain in the Battle of Towton Field. The Machells of Crackenthorpe must also have been at Towton, on Palm Sunday, March 29, 1461. The battle was the biggest and bloodiest of the Wars of the Roses and secured the throne for Edward IV, the king who later gave a pardon to John Machell.

The Lancastrian King Henry VI, after his defeat at the battle of Hexham, was given shelter at Crackenthorpe by John Machell and his wife Katherine. Legend has it that he was disguised as a gardener when Yorkist troops came looking for him.

Dr John Lingard (1771-1851) a Roman Catholic priest who was also a celebrated historian, noted: "Henry VI was frequently concealed in the house of John Machell of Crackenthorpe..."

Historian Cresswell, on his visit to Crackenthorpe, noted: "There is a room in the Hall known as the King's Bedchamber, the garden on the other side of the road opposite the entrance gates, is known as the King's Garden."

Loyal service to a monarch indeed. So what was the reason

for Mistress Machell's fury when she rode out with her ghostly retinue?

Locals claimed that she had been cheated out of her share of the estate. It certainly seemed so! When her husband Lancelot died in 1686 she was made an executrix. She must have had a face like thunder when she heard of the bequests. Elizabeth was at the bottom of the list!

Lancelot had first left two pictures to his son Hugh, then to his grandson Lancelot, and then to the heirs of his family.

One was of Anne, Countess of Pembroke, given to Lancelot by the lady herself, the other was of Lord George, Earl of Cumberland, father of the Countess, originally given to the late Lancelot by Richard, Earl of Thanet. In 1656 Lancelot had become one of the trustees of the estate at Temple Sowerby purchased by the Dowager Countess of Pembroke. The Countess who had a particular respect for the Machell family "who for upwards of 500 years, as she herself affirmed, had served in the retinue of her family."

Hugh and Lancelot were to also inherit all the furniture and their other bequest included a plate bearing the family arms and a leather gilded Bible carrying the King's Arms.

The late Lancelot's daughter-in-law Elisabeth was to have twenty shillings to buy a ring. Reginald Hill, for his kindness during Lancelot's illness, received forty shillings, as did servants William Brunskill and Anne Bousfield. A Thomas Fawcett was to receive his black suit and coat.

Then, and only then, did his wife get a mention! The will ended: "To my wife Elizabeth Machell, my son Thomas Machell and my daughter Susan Machell the rest of my goods and I appoint them as executors."

In 1786, two years before his death, another Lancelot Machell, unmarried, sold the manor and the last 328 acres of the estate, bringing to an end 600 years of occupation by the family.

There are but few remnants. David Balfour told me of one, the splendid four-poster that once graced a bedroom at Crackenthorpe that is now on display in London's Victoria and Albert museum.

In 1887, over 100 years later, a Captain Machell bought back Crackenthorpe, restoring the old portion and adding a new house. Its terraced garden leads down to a tree-shaded footpath which, in turn winds down a steep bank to the edge of the River Eden. On the day I visited the sunlit waters were tumbling over the stone under which Peg reputedly lies.

In 1975 the head of the family was a Montague Arthur Machell, living in Phoenix, Arizona!

Enough, surely, to send Peg Sneddle into yet another of her tantrums?

It's a haunting thought!

Rydal Mount

Rydal Mount, tucked into a corner of the very heart of Lakeland, has been a home for many families over the past five hundred years. In 1574 it was a yeoman's dwelling on the fringe of Ambleside, owned by a John Keene. Over the years it grew from cottage to splendid house, but its most famous residents were the Wordsworth family.

It was to be the setting for many a human drama. Loves were won and lost; children were born and, sadly, children were to die; friendships were cemented, others were to crumble for ever; passions were fuelled by drink and drugs. Tragedy, or so it seemed, was always around the corner.

It was in 1813 that the poet William Wordsworth rented the house from Lady Diana le Fleming of nearby Rydal Hall, widow of Sir Michael and the daughter of Thomas, 14th Earl of Suffolk. William found he could afford the rent of the house close by Rydal Water after Lord Lonsdale had procured for him the sinecure post of Distributor of Stamps. The Wordsworths and their entourage moved in on May Day 1813. Leaving behind Allan Bank, a cold, draughty and smoky house in Grasmere, were William, wife Mary (nee Hutchinson), their surviving three children, John (9), Dora (7) and William junior, just two years old. With them came Wordsworth's sister Dorothy and his sister-in-law Sarah Hutchinson. It was to be 46 years before Wordsworth's widow Mary, the last of them, died there in 1859.

Rydal Mount, the house that knew so much love and laughter yet so much sadness, so many tears and frustrations, must be haunted by memories. In 1856 a young girl, Mary - a member of a family which enjoyed a lifelong friendship with the Wordsworths - experienced an odd feeling about the house. She had been taken there by her grandmother, wife of Dr Thomas Arnold, the famous headmaster of Rugby School and friend of Wordsworth who had built a holiday home, Fox How, nearby. Wordsworth, who had helped Arnold with the design of the house, had died six years earlier, his widow was still alive.

Mary - who was later to become Mrs Humphry Ward - recorded events later in life in her book A Writers Recollections which was published in 1918.

"I can vividly recollect sitting on a footstool at Mrs Wordsworth's feet," she wrote. I still see the little room with its plain furniture, the chair beside the fire and the old lady in it. I can still recall the childish feeling that this was no common visit, and the house no common house - that a presence still haunted it."

Later Mary's own daughter was to see something more substantial.

In fact it was 52 years later, in September, 1911, that Mary, now Mrs Humphry Ward, returned to stay for a few weeks as tenant of Rydal Mount. Two days later she was joined by her husband and eldest daughter.

It was that eldest daughter who recorded the strange story thus:

"Last night, my first in Rydal Mount, I slept in the corner room, over the small sitting room. I had drawn up the blind about

halfway up the window before going to bed, and had drawn the curtain aside, over the back of a wooden armchair that stood against the window. The window, a casement, was wide open.

"I slept soundly, but woke quite suddenly, at what hour I do not know, and found myself sitting bolt upright in bed looking towards the window. Very bright moonlight was shining into the room and I could just see the corner of Laughing out in the distance.

"My first impression was of bright moonlight, but then I became strongly conscious of the moonlight striking on something and I saw perfectly clearly the figure of an old man sitting in the armchair by the window.

"I said to myself - 'That's Wordsworth!'

"He was sitting with either hand resting on the arms of the chair, leaning back, his head rather bent and he seemed to be looking down, straight in front of him with a rapt expression. He was not looking at me, nor out the window.

"The moonlight lit up the top of his head and the silvery hair and I noticed the hair was very thin. The whole impression was of something solemn and beautiful and I was not in the least frightened.

As I looked - I cannot say when I looked again, for I have no recollection of ceasing to look or looking away - the figure disappeared and I became aware of the empty chair.

"I lay back again and thought for a moment in a pleased and contented way - 'That was Wordsworth!' ' ”

She made no claim for it to be of a supernatural origin and a member of the Psychical Society dismissed it as a visual hallucination. However, it was not till afterwards they discovered that she had been sleeping in Dorothy's old room in which she (Dorothy) spent so many pain-wracked hours. In that very corner by the window William must have sat, day after day, when visiting the tragic sister who had been the inspiration of his youth.

Dorothy Wordsworth had her share of joy and sorrow, sadly ending her days in a twilight world. As a six-year-old, after the death of her parents, she was torn from her beloved brothers and sent to live for seven years with friends near Halifax. Later she was to become a constant companion and inspiration for William but in 1814 she seemed to be edged out again, spending just three months with her brother, a dramatic change from the previous 20 years. For the next few years there were to be constant separations.

The tone of William's letters changed. Gone were 'how I miss you passionately' and 'how long till we meet.' 'Beloved' also disappeared, replaced with everyday matters and household gossip.

Thomas De Quincey, a family friend and constant visitor to Rydal Mount, described Dorothy thus: "Her face was of Egyptian brown; rarely, in a woman of English birth, had I seen a more determinate gypsy tan. Her eyes were not soft, as Mrs Wordsworth's, nor were they fierce or bold; but they were wild and startling, and hurried in their motion. Her manner was warm and even ardent...”

Her conversation had, said De Quincey: “ ... an air of embarrassment and even of self conflict that was sometimes distressing to witness. Even her very utterance and enunciation often, or generally, suffered in point of clearness and steadiness from the agitation of her excessive organic sensibility, and, perhaps, from some morbid irri-

tability of the nerves."

How prescient he was! Poor Dorothy. Ernest De Selincourt, in his biography, said of her: "Since girlhood the effort to maintain control over so full an emotional life, affections so tender and passionate, sensibilities so acute, had entailed a constant drain upon her nervous energy."

For 64 years she dedicated herself to providing loving care for family and friends. She kept a journal of daily doings; it was she who inspired part of William's 'Daffodils'.

"Her physique, never robust, had bravely responded to the call; then the onset and successive shocks of a severe illness destroyed the delicate adjustment of mind and body; and Nature chose to preserve the worn-out physical frame by releasing it from the most exacting demands upon it," said De Selincourt.

Dorothy became insane. Two weeks after her collapse William, writing to his diarist/lawyer friend Henry Crabb Robinson, confessed: "I fear that you cannot read this letter. My hand is shaking. I have had so much agitation today in attempting to quiet my poor sister and from the necessity of refusing her things which would be improper for her."

In 1836, Mary Wordsworth, wrote: "Dear Dorothy is now asleep after having been half an hour in the garden; on going out she wept aloud like a baby, being overcome with the beauty around her, and asked to be taken to a certain border. At first she was too over-powered to look at it then she became to sing."

A year later Mary Wordsworth told her friend Catherine Clarkson: "Distressing as her state is, more especially to those who know what she once was, it is a comfort to see that she is happy - that is she has no distress or sorrow that oppresses her more than the tran-sient sorrow of a spoilt child - to such as one we can only liken her. Yet at times if you can fix her attention, her intellect is as bright, and she will express an opinion when asked, with as much judgement as in her best days - but alas these gleams are short-lived.

"Her restless feelings (which we attribute to something going on in the head which she rubs perpetually) prevent her finding quiet for reading - nor will she often listen to it - she says she is too busy with her own feelings! And thus, dear friend, she wears away the day. Her greatest discomforts proceed from habits that I cannot describe - it would be too painful for us both were I to attempt it."

In her more lucid moments Dorothy put pen to paper, on October 8, 1837, writing to Edward Ferguson, companion of her girl-hood days in Halifax: "A madman might as well attempt to relate the history of his own doings, and those of his fellows in confinement, as I to tell you one hundredth part of what I have felt, suffered, and done. Through God's mercy I am now calm and easy."

She had to wait another eighteen years before being released from her unhappy state. Dorothy, nursed faithfully by her sister in law Mary Hutchinson, died at Rydal Mount in 1855.

Certainly others would have reason to haunt the house of memories.

One would be little Dora, William and Mary's daughter, whose life was dogged by latent tuberculosis.

In 1841, aged 35, she was married late in life to a widower, years older, Edward Quillinan, a retired Irish Dragoon, and spent her honeymoon at Rydal Mount. The couple lived for a short time in Portugal for her health but in 1847 came home to die at Rydal Mount of galloping consumption. She was just 43.

Her illness had not been improved by catching a chill whilst visiting the village of Brisco, near Carlisle, where she was looking over a cottage for her brother Willy. He had married Fanny Elizabeth Graham in Brighton but was to live in the North. On August 29, 1851, their son William was christened in St Mary's in Carlisle.

Dora had had a long wait for a husband. She had been 17 when first they met. He was then a man of 30, wed, and with two children, a family friend of William Wordsworth and his sister who came to Rydal on visits. In 1822 it was Dorothy who nursed Mrs Quillinan in her final illness. Four years later Dora confessed to a friend, "I like the dear heavy dragoon better than any man", but had to wait 11 years before William was asked to consent to their engagement and another four years before the wedding. Tragically she was to die just six years later.

She had been a favourite of William, becoming his devoted companion, accompanying him on many of his tours.

After her death he was inconsolable: "She is ever with me, and will be to the last moment of my life."

Then again, perhaps the spirit of Sara Hutchinson, who died on June 23, 1835, aged 60, could be loathe to leave Rydal Mount. She was heartbroken by the death of the man she loved - William's sailor brother John, who perished at sea. His ship, the Earl of Abergavenny, on the East Indies run, was caught in a gale off Portland Bill and sank off the coast of Dorset on February 5, 1805.

The early death of their parents had led to the breaking up of the Wordsworth family. In later years William was the good shepherd, caring for his family flock. Now John was dead. William wrote to his brother Richard: "We wish you were with us. God keep the rest of us together. The set is now broken."

To life-time friend James Losh, with whom he had been at

Cambridge, he wrote: "Oh! My friend I shall never forget him! His image, if my senses remain, will be with me at my last hour and I will endeavour to die as he did, and what is of still more consequence perhaps, to live as he did..."

Step forward Thomas De Quincey, another player who strode the Wordsworth stage. One-time brilliant editor of the Westmoreland Gazette and self-confessed opium eater; he was a literary man who later was to know so many of the family secrets.

He had hero-worshipped William. In 1805 he travelled to the Lakes in the hope of meeting the poet but his nerve gave way. The next year he returned, reached Dove Cottage, but was too embarrassed to introduce himself. In 1807 he heard that Wordsworth and Coleridge were in London, but missed seeing them. The same year, whilst staying with his mother in Bristol, he heard that Coleridge was at nearby Nether Stowey and eventually met him there. He became very close to the family, and when Coleridge was busy lecturing in London it was De Quincey who escorted Mrs Coleridge and her three children on their visit to Wordsworth at Grasmere and Southey at Greta Hall.

Wordsworth shook his hand. His dream had come true. He had met his hero. The next morning he found a kettle bubbling over the fire and Dorothy making breakfast, after which he joined brother and sister for a six-mile walk around Rydal and Grasmere.

After his return to London De Quincey kept up a correspondence with the women of the Wordsworth circle, exchanging gossip and family news. Most of all he loved to hear about the children, buying them pictures and books.

His favourite was Catherine, baby of the family, who died in June, 1812. She had one convulsion the year before. She was just four years old when she had her last.

De Quincey had loved the child and became mentally deranged after hearing of her death.

Every night for two months he stretched himself out over the grave of his beloved Katie in Grasmere churchyard where she had happily played only the day before her death.

Just six months later tragedy struck again: in December, her little brother Thomas died, developing pneumonia after catching measles. He was just six and a half years old.

Frustrated and shattered lives, tragedies galore. Reason enough for any haunting of Rydal Mount.

It was home to so many talented and gifted people, a setting for so much happiness. But it also had its share of so many problems and so much sadness.

Haunted or not?

Perhaps it is only wonderful memories that live on!

Sir James Lowther

It was June 9, 1802. Overhead a summer sun shone down on Lowther's St Michael's Church standing in The Park on the east bank of the River Lowther. The bell, cast in 1687 by William Eldridge in Chertsey, and hanging in the belfry that stands a little way from the church, had tolled its summons. Mourners' horses had been tethered to the belfry and they were now seated, their eyes wandering aloft to the splendid cupola - added in 1686 by Sir John Lowther - that capped the Saxon and Norman pillars and arches. To each side of them were the chapels filled with memorials to the Lowthers.

The Reverend William Lowther, BA., was in full flow, the obsequies, praise to the late departed, religiously observed, for was this not the funeral of Sir James Lowther, the first Lord Lonsdale? He had died on May 2, aged sixty-six.

Not only a wealthy landowner as well as owner of the hugely profitable West Cumbrian coal pits, he was a man who had played his part - though at many timers dubiously - in the politics of the North-west corner of England. It was all so correct.

THEN, SUDDENLY, THE PULPIT STARTED ROCKING!

In 1857 Jeremiah Sullivan, in his book "Cumberland and Westmorland, Ancient and Modern", risked the wrath of the Lonsdale family, writing: "Westmorland never produced a more famous boggle - infamous as a man, famous as a boggle - than Jemmy Lowther, well-known, for want of a more appropriate name, as the "The bad Lord Lonsdale". This notorious character, who seemed the transmigration of the worst and coarsest feudal baron ever imported into England by the Conqueror, became a still greater terror to the country after death, than he had been during his life. He was with great difficulty buried; and whilst the clergyman was praying over him, he nearly knocked the reverend gentleman from his desk.. When placed in the grave , the power of creating alarm was not interred with his bones."

The Reverend William Lowther, inducted into the rectory of Lowther on August 26, 1769, must have been aghast.

If the legend is correct Sullivan was right. What was to later follow was terrifying. There were disturbances in the Hall, noises in the stables at Lowther Castle, and neither men nor animals could rest.

Sullivan's account went on: "There is nothing said of his shape, or whether he appeared at all; but it is certain he made himself audible. The Hall became almost uninhabitable, and out of doors there was always the danger of meeting the miscreant ghost."

Many years ago a man born in Penrith, but by then living in Carlisle, recalled that his grandfather often told him tales of a ghostly coach, drawn by four wild horses, that would come rushing madly from the gates of the castle and along the road to Penrith. The coach was supposed to have been carrying the spirit of the first Lord Lonsdale.

The tale goes that so much terror followed that a priest eventually had him laid under a large rock called Wallow Crag that overlooked Haweswater, and by so doing appears to have laid his ghost for ever. Others had it that his body was disinterred and reburied on Hugh Laithes Pike - close by the Wallow Crag.

But then again, the Earl's lifestyle was hardly normal.

Thomas De Quincey, editor of the Westmorland Gazette during 1818/19, said of him: "He was a true feudal chieftain, and in the approaches to his mansion, in the style of his equipage, or whatever else was likely to meet the human eye, he delighted to express disdain to modern refinement by the haughty carelessness of his magnificence.

"The coach in which he used to visit Penrith was old and neglected; his horses fine and untrimmed, and such was the impression diffused about him, by his gloomy temper and fits of oppression, that, according to a Penrith contemporary of the old despot, the streets were silent as he traversed them and awe sat upon many faces."

If the description was accurate, one can well understand that the good folk of Penrith and Lowther had many tales to tell of the eccentric lord, born on August 5, 1735, created an Earl on May 24, 1784, and who, in London, was constantly fighting duels.

At one time he lived in Stanwix House in Carlisle's Fisher Street and caused a political scandal when, between September 1784 and February, 1785, he created almost 1,500 of his miners Freemen, allowing them a vote in the election and ensuring a "yellow victory" in 1788. His nicknames included Jemmy the Bad Earl, Old Thunder, and Jimmy Grasp-all, Earle of Toadstool.

John Christian Curwen, later MP for Workington and the man, along with Charles Howard, Earl of Surrey, credited with rescuing the Carlisle seat from the grasp of the Lowthers, pulled no punches in a 1790 election handbill on behalf of independent candidates. He declared: "The opponents (Sir James & co) scarcely deserve the name of a party, they are the tools of a despicable tyrant, who is odious if we consider the object of his attempts, contemptible and ridiculous if we look at the general event of them. Under such a leader we can expect nothing that is generous, nothing that is manly; his friends are indefatigable in the arts of corruption..."

One tale has it that Sir James fell in love with a woman - but no aristocrat or lady of the county - that he had met casually. He talked her into living with him and rented a fine house in Hampshire.

Who she was, whether she really loved him, or was happy with such splendour, is not known, but when she came seriously ill and died, so great was his distress that no-one later dared to mention her whilst talking to him.

Worse, he refused to have her body buried. When servants complained about the smell from the decaying corpse he sacked them. Eventually the body was placed in a tomb and the unhappy nobleman mourned for his beloved until his dying day.

Legend has it that he kept her head in a glass case.

It is no wonder that Alexander Carlyle, the Scottish minister who knew many of the literary giants of the day, once exclaimed: "He was more detested than any man alive, as a shameless political sharper, a domestic bashaw and an intolerant tyrant over his tenants and dependants." In Carlyle's opinion Sir James was "Truly a madman, but too rich to be confined!"

MP, writer and publisher Horace Walpole, nephew of the famous politician, was no more flattering, saying that Sir James was

"Equally unamiable in public and private." The description would be accurate, for Walpole was a man said to be a wit, virtuoso and man of quality. Contemporaries said: "His critical taste was good."

If the pulpit had really rocked there appears to be no record of it doing so. The Earl's death was recorded in simple fashion in the Carlisle Journal. It read: "On Monday evening, at his seat at Lowther Hall, in the 64th year of his age, the Right Honourable James, Earl of Lonsdale." But again, the paper, then consisting of just four pages, had more important national and international news to use in the limited space available. There would be no room for idle tittle tattle about hauntings - they would be ignored!

But despite living in grandeur at Lowther Park Sir James was certainly a miserly curmudgeon, one on whom the local gossips could seize as ideal subject matter.

Joseph Farington, the artist who lived from 1747-1821, was a constant visitor to the area, being best-known for his engraved views of the Lakes. "The Earl," he said, "was an exacting landlord, he lived parsimoniously, sending to Penrith, it is said, for wine merely by the dozen, and of very inferior quality, when entertaining the Assize judges every year, although he was said to have left a vast stock of wine worth £10,000 at his death."

In contrast he persevered to the last in spending vast sums to win control of Carlisle at election time. In the July after his death 9,000 guineas were in his bureau, set aside for the forthcoming struggle."

The lady whose head he was said to have kept in a glass case? If the tale is true it must have been in his early years, for on September 7, 1761, Sir James had married Lady Mary Stewart, daughter of John, Earl of Bute, by Lady Wortley Montague, only daughter of Edward Wortley Montague, Ambassador to Constantinople. She died, aged 86, in Fulham in 1824. They had no children.

Sizergh Castle

In days of old when knights were bold they were also exceedingly mistrusting. Before setting off for distant battles and spending months, possibly even years, away from home, these warriors of old often locked their wives safely away.

Sir Walter Strickland, whose Sizergh castle is set in wooded parkland on the road from Milnthorpe to Kendal, was one such man. But it was to be a fate much worse than temporary discomfort which faced his lady.

On June 28, 1537, King Henry VIII gave Sir Walter a Royal Commission. He was to help Sir Thomas Wharton, Deputy Warden of the Western Marches - the lands that straddled the England Scotland border - and Thomas Wentworth, Captain of Carlisle Castle and city, to keep the peace in the turbulent borderlands. The aptly named Debateable Lands.

The Stricklands had a habit of going off to war. Sir John De Stirkeland, living at Sizergh in 1344, was to be found in the French and Scottish wars. In 1415 Sir Thomas De Strickland was at Agincourt, as was his brother William, a

75

Lancer in Sir John Nevill's retinue. Sir Walter would have been at the Battle of Solway Moss which followed the 1542 invasion by a Scots army that marched out of Lochmaben and through Gretna to cross the River Esk and attack the outskirts of Carlisle.

Sir Walter was part of the English army under Sir Thomas Wharton which defeated the marauders. A mere 1,000 plus force overthrew the 15,000 strong Scots; a victory in which they were aided by the Scots refusal to fight under the command of the despised General Oliver Sinclair. It helps if the opposition do not fight as well they might.

Sir Walter Strickland, descendant of an ancient family dating back to 1215 and the days of King John, may well have gazed proudly at the spoils of victory that included 1,000 prisoners, 24 cannon, four cartloads of spears and ten splendid pavilions. He would also be aware that back home at Sizergh Castle his young wife Margaret, daughter of Sir Stephen Hammerston, was locked away; presumably in both senses of the word. She was under age when first contracted in marriage in 1535. And before leaving to carry out the King's commission - which was rewarded with a pension for life - he had confined her in the top storey of the castle's pele tower.

Sizergh was a formidable fortress, typical of the old manorial homes of Northern England. The tower in which Margaret was a virtual prisoner was 60 feet high, measured 60 feet by 39 and a half feet and had walls seven feet thick pierced with six loopholes.

The servants had been warned that Margaret was not to be allowed out of the chamber that lay off an open gallery reached only by a spiral staircase. Legend has it that, terrified of Sir Walter, the servants (rather bizarrely) dared not even open the door to feed her. Her screams, muffled by the solid walls, were apparently ignored and the lady actually starved to death.

It would seem that the Hammerston family were cursed - Margaret's father, Sir Stephen, was executed for joining the Aske Revolution, part of which, in October 1536, was the 'Pilgrimage of Grace' protesting at King Henry VIII's suppression of the smaller

monasteries.

And it was Margaret's ghost that was to disturb later guests at Sizergh. Legend has it that screams echoed through the building and the floor boards in the room in which she had been incarcerated would be found lifted time and time again.

In 1888 Michael Taylor MD, a Fellow of the Society of Antiquarians - and, as a doctor of medicine obviously a level headed man - was showing a party of fellow antiquarians around Sizergh. Before climbing to the third storey of the tower he told them: "The chamber we are about to visit is the proverbial haunted room of the castle; it is redolent of ghosts - supernatural sounds are heard, the boards won't lay quiet in their place, the hair of the deceased lady still clings to the wall - all the attributes are there of a very respectable ghost chamber."

Another highly respected visitor was Edward Bellasis, a barrister who was also Lancaster Herald of the College of Arms. In a paper published in the Transactions of the Cumberland & Westmoreland Antiquarian and Archaeological Society he said: "There is a lumber room on the third floor known as Madame Hammerston's Room. Every respectable family seems to like the possession of a ghost, at least so long as it does not become too troublesome of a night. Mysterious rumours reach me as to this room being haunted, since here Mistress Hammerston met her fate, was murdered and so on.

"The ghostly theory - albeit misty as it ought to be - has thus much in its favour, that, were it a sham, that is to say a substantial burglar in the concrete and it not the poetical abstraction that tradition loves so well, would surely never have been content up there so long, doing no good business whatever. It would have seized occasion for dives into the excellent cellar and plentiful larder below!"

John F. Curwen, another Fellow of the Antiquarian Society, confirmed the story when describing Sizergh Castle, saying: "The balcony, which is modern, leads to the ghost chamber on the South-east side of the tower."

A haunted tower? Two facts are irrefutable. First, murdered or starved to death, Margaret Hammerston died soon. Her death was early enough to allow Sir Walter to marry twice more. Secondly, at least three eminent and sensible Victorians confirmed that there was a haunted chamber in Sizergh Castle. A sketch of the layout of the building by John Curwen shows the position of the haunted chamber.

And why has is it been known throughout the centuries as Mistress Hammerston's Room?

Sir Walter Strickland wed Agnes as his second wife, and on January 30, 1560, he married Alice, the daughter of Nicholas Tempest from Stanley, in County Durham. Surely worn out by battles, hauntings and three wives in the space of 34 years, he died on April 8, 1569.

His widow, Alice, remarried, first Sir Christopher Place, then, after being widowed again, in 1573 she wed Sir Thomas Boynton, the 50-year old Sheriff of Yorkshire. Eight years later he was dead.

It was Alice who, as Lady Boynton, carried out extensive decorative work in the tower - to this day there is a "Boynton Room" much admired by architectural expert Nicholas Pevenser - and the castle, left to her for life, was eventually released to Thomas, her son by Sir Walter.

She was luckier by far than the tragic Margaret.

Who could blame her ghost for screaming and ripping up the floor boards!

Nick Shire, House Manager at Sizergh Castle, said that while locking up the castle late at night and knowing that he is the only person in the castle at that time he has actually heard footsteps in the chamber directly above. In the two years or so he has been at the castle this has happened on a number of occasions.

Goggle-eyed Ghost Boggled the Vicar

The vicar was at the end of one of his charitable rounds as he trudged the road from Sawrey to Hawkshead and was approaching the cottage at Waterside that in those days served as the Poor-house for Claife. It was a night in early Spring and a snow shower had laid a gleaming coat of white on the path that edged the eastern bank of Esthwaite Water.

Very soon he noticed a figure on the road ahead of him, and, as he caught up with it, asumed from the clothing that it was a woman. Also believing her to be one of his parishioners, he bade her "good night".

There was no reply. He turned to see just who the unsociable traveller was and staggered back in horror. Later he was to tell friends: "Under a broad-brimmed bonnet there I saw a death-like countenance with goggle eyes that gleamed like coloured glass with a light behind them."

The apparition then stepped off the road to disappear through a gap in the wall. Astonished, the vicar stepped up to the wall, but no trace of the figure was to be found. He looked back along the road. The moon was full and by its bright light he saw something that sent shivers down his back. THE SNOW BORE ONLY ONE SET OF FOOTPRINTS - AND THEY WERE HIS OWN!

The story has to be believed. It came from the most respectable of sources - the horrified man himself. He was the Reverend George Park, from 1834 until 1865 the vicar of St Michael's Church in Hawkshead.

In 1896 local historian Henry Swainson Cowper, after investigating local tales of mysterious happenings, reported: "There are, however, certain localities which have long had a bad reputation, which, indeed, clings to most of them, and in some of these there are not a few living people who can say something on the subject.

"It is very curious that the road which runs on the margin of

Esthwaite, on every side, is badly haunted in several places. The most widely known and least explicable, however, is the Waterside Boggle which has frightened many an honest man on the road between Lake Field and the cottage at Waterside which was at one time the Claife Poorhouse.

Cowper added: "One of the most practical farmers in the locality, and a man eminently unsuperstitious, informed me that the most remarkable thing about the place was the fact that cattle often became panic-struck with terror near the Poorhouse and could be hardly got to pass it."

So did vicars have a direct line to the world of ghosties and ghouls? It would seem so. Cowper, a Hawkshead man, had a paper published in the Transactions of the Cumberland and Westmorland Archaeological and Antiquarian Society, which also told of Bellmount, a haunted house at the Northern end of Windermere.

It had been built by the Reverend Reginald Braithwaite, who in 1774 was the then vicar of Hawkshead and a descendent of the family of that name of Ambleside Hall.

It was to prove a far from peaceful haven for the minister. Said Cowper: "Servants living in the house heard fearful sounds in the night. In the morning all the doors were found to be thrown open. Travellers at night saw windows brilliantly lit when the house was known to be empty. One woman told Cowper she had seen a securely locked gate fly open as she passed by, ramblers whose curiosity led them to peer through the windows claimed to have seen an apparition which appeared as a tall woman dressed all in white.

But then the good folk of Hawkshead were no strangers to hauntings, witches and strange goings-on; that there should be so many ghosts would seem not so unusual.

Another tale was set on a dark and stormy night in he late 1500's. A party of travellers were resting at The Ferry House, a tavern standing by the Windermere waterside when a loud and repeated cry for a boat was heard from the Ferry Nab.

A ferryman, a quiet and sober person, answered the call and

in the teeth of a gale rowed across the lake. After allowing time for the passage to and from the far shore the tavern guests stepped outside to meet the boatman and see who was the belated traveller. There was no passenger. The boatman was alone, horror-stricken with a ghastly look upon his face. Worse, he had been struck dumb with fright.

The next morning found him in a high fever and he continued speechless for several days at the end of which he died. He had given no explanation of what he had seen at the Nab.

For long afterwards, on every stormy night, the same unearthly yell was heard echoing across the lake, accompanied by weird shouts and howls. No boatman would answer any call after dark and travellers began to avoid the ferry.

So serious was the matter that a monk, summoned from Furness Abbey, was instructed to exorcise the ghost. On a Christmas Day he assembled the inhabitants on Chapel Island and a religious ceremony was performed by which the ghost was to be ever confined within the desolate quarry on Latterbrow Heights.

More gruesome were the events of April 18, 1672. Parish records tell the story: "Thomas Lancaster, who for poysonning his owne family was adjudged at the Assizes at Lancaster to be carried back to his owne house at High Wray, where he lived, and was there hanged before his owne door till he was dead and then was brought in with horse and carriage on the Coulthouse Meadow and forthwith hung up in iron chaynes on a gibbet which was set for that purpose on the south side of Sawrey Cassy near unto the Pool Stang and there continued until such time he was rotted away for bone."

Plenty of reasons for ghosts galore! And no wonder the Reverend Park met up with a disappearing goggle-eyed lady!

Dalston Hall

Cumbria is renowned for its glorious Lake District; the grandeur of its mountains, the majesty of its lakes - and the proximity of the Roman Wall - attracts visitors from the world over.

But many of them will never know of the other visitors - the ghosts that haunt the ancient houses of the county. The spectres come from many periods of history.

Dalston Hall Hotel, just a few miles outside the city of Carlisle, is a good example.

It was early evening when the glasses slid slowly to the edge of the restaurant bar. One by one, they fell to the floor and smashed.

The two waitresses, setting tables, turned in surprise. They then froze in horror. There was no-one behind the bar - no human hand had been behind the goblets!

It was 1997. Soon after the eerie happening the fire alarm sounded. There was no fire! But a blaze DID almost destroy the restaurant area a few weeks later.

Jane Thompson, owner of the hotel, thinks that the earlier incidents were the work of the hotel's most regular ghost, known to her and manager Lisa Avey as 'Lady Jane'.

Said the present-day Jane: "I think she was trying to warn us of the fire".

Who knows? Perhaps the ephemeral Lady Jane was also much concerned over the prospect of losing her favourite haunt!

Said Jane: " She is the one most often seen by the guests who stay here."

Certainly the Lady could well be an upper-class apparition; Dalston Hall has a long and varied history.

In 1875 Carlisle architect Charles Ferguson was fulsome in his praise of the building approached through an avenue of magnificent beech trees, saying: "It has a commanding position and can be seen for miles around. Its mellow-tinted walls and graceful composition ever lends a charm to the landscape."

In the early 1400's it had been a simple pele tower but over the centuries had developed into a building of some splendour.

No less splendid was the Dalston family who had lived there since the early fifteenth century. In 1612, in the reign of Charles I, Sir John Dalston was High Sheriff of Cumberland. Six years later his son, Sir George, was the next High Sheriff.

Sir John and Sir George were said to be "both brave, gentile, gallants and justicians, great gamesters, and never without two or three running horses, the best in England".

For almost forty years Sir George was also an MP for Cumberland. He was also a regular member of the congregation at nearby Dalston church. It was said: "He would be there so early that he was seen to walk in the churchyard before prayers, ready to confess his sin at the beginning and for the blessing at the end of prayers."

He died at an old age - in the midst of friends and in the midst of a prayer!

The bishops of Carlisle owned Dalston Hall. Those who lived there were "bond" tenants. Old Sir John Dalston made many attempts to end the agreement. In December 1696 a great flood created chaos in the area, breaching the weirs and dams that controlled the water supply to the local mills.

The mills, without water, were useless. Sir John continued to refuse to pay his £10 share. The Bishop gave in, paying it himself instead of the crafty old knight!

During the Civil War siege of Carlisle in 1664 General David Leslie made his headquarters at Dalston Hall. Sir George's son, Sir William, was one of the leading Royalists and was later created Baronet by a grateful King Charles II. The days of Cavaliers and Roundheads, plots and counter-plots surely must have provided some of the ghosts that haunt the hall today.

In 1761 Dalston Hall, by then a fine old mansion and estate, was sold by the last Sir George. Today it is a fine residential hotel, restaurant, venue for many functions ... and, as well as Lady Jane, home to a whole collection of ghosts.

Manager Lisa Avey is no stranger to the other world of spirits. When working at the Cumbria Hotel in Carlisle - now the Lakes Court - she was locking up and had to pass through the cellars to reach the main hotel building. An area of freezing cold air suddenly enveloped her. She never walked the cellars alone again.

Jane Thompson will tell you of the Grey Lady of Abbey

Street - one of Carlisle's oldest thoroughfares... It is no surprise that they can coolly recount ghostly tales of Dalston Hall.

Jane, as well as at least one guest, has heard the sound of children's laughter coming from the foot of the old Pele tower stairs. The worn stone steps spiral up to what is now the top-storey Honeymoon Suite - THE LAUGHTER CAME FROM EMPTY SPACE

One pair of newly-weds who stayed in the honeymoon suite told how the husband, who was taking a shower, saw, out of the corner of his eye, a figure passing the bed. He thought it was his wife. Returning to the room he found her still in bed.

SHE HAD NOT LEFT IT WHILST HE WAS SHOWERING!

Jane Thompson has heard the sound of barrels being rolled across the cellar floors.

ON INVESTIGATION SHE FOUND NO-ONE THERE,

Marion Goodfellow, a member of a TV team making a ghost-busting film at the hall claims to have seen a man in a smoking jacket in Room 7. The aroma of cigars filled the room. When she looked again he had disappeared!

But the most frequently haunted part of the hall has to be Room 4. It is here that mostly men have eerie experiences. Manager Lisa and hubby Martin spent a night in Room 4. Says Lisa: "There were no bad vibes but we woke up in the night with the feeling that there was some-one in the room watching us.

"We went back to sleep but in the morning Martin asked me whether I had had a good sleep. He told me he had woken up two or three times more - with the feeling that there was definitely something in the room.

It was in that room that ghostbuster Marion Goodfellow did sense a presence. SHE TOLD JANE AND LISA THAT SHE HAD SEEN A YOUNG WOMAN MATERIALISING THROUGH THE WALL.

Another guest who had stayed in Room 6 told how, on going to bed he had put out the light but soon after, by the moonlight shin-

ing through the blinds saw woman with long dark hair sitting smiling at him. Other guests have had the same experience. They have told how the apparition seems to come from the wardrobe and then either sits on the bed or gets into bed with them!

Jane tells of the Dalston doctor who, driving past the hall, saw a woman in Victorian clothes floating around the garden. He saw her twice. After that he took a different route.

That Dalston Hall is haunted is not all that surprising. Just up the road the village of Dalston has seen mysterious deaths over the centuries.

October 13, 1577, was unlucky thirteen for Elizabeth Nixon - a member of a family described as "rude Borderers. She hung herself.

January 24 the previous year had seen Vidva Brown drown herself. The same year Richard Burns hanged himself, eighteen days later John Feddon, a pauper, was found hanged, his body swinging from the church bell-rope.

On December 19, ten-years-old John Smith was found dead on the Bishop's Dyke, close by Dalston Hall. On June 17, 1583, Anthony Tickell fell off his horse whilst asleep and died, and in September 1585, the Dalston Parish Register recorded the death of infant Thomas Reyson - slain by a door. A whole host of recruits for a ghostly army!

Perhaps the young ladies who ended it all by drowning were just a little luckier than one other ghost of Dalston Hall - the tragic young girl who, legend has it, came to a nasty end - thrown down the steep and twisting stairs of the old pele tower!